My People

Are Destroyed for Lack of Knowledge

A Biblical Account
in
Chart Form

by
Jackie Fowler

Fowler Enterprises
Tulsa, Oklahoma

Unless otherwise noted, all Scripture quotations are from the *King James Version* of the Bible.

Scriptures marked GNB are from the *Good News Bible, Today's English Version*, copyright © American Bible Society 1966, 1971, 1976.

3rd Printing
Over 21,000 in Print

My People
Are Destroyed for Lack of Knowledge
A Biblical Account in Chart Form
ISBN 0-9633722-0-3
Copyright ©1991 by Jackie Fowler
TXU 489-882
P. O. Box 1327
Tulsa, Oklahoma 74101

Dedicated To . . .

Seeking the Lost Ministry — *for without their knowledge, this book could not have been written.*

My Husband, Leon — *for without his love and support, this book would not have been completed.*

My children, LaKeisha and Leon II — *who inspired me to seek out our biblical heritage.*

My parents, Rev. and Mrs. Frank Manning — *who believed in this book.*

*And Last but not least, to the **King of kings and Lord of lords, Jesus Christ,** Who placed this book in my heart to write.*

Contents

Preface: A Parable

One day a boy found a baby wolf in the woods. The boy decided to take him home and raise him up with the other puppies. As time went by, the cub grew up to act like the other dogs. He was tame, house-broken, and the family pet. This wolf did everything he saw the other dogs do. Why? Because he didn't know his behavior as a wolf was different from that of a dog.

Sometimes at night the wolf would awake and walk around and hear wolves howling in the distant night air. This went on, night after night. Soon the boy began to notice a difference in the way the wolf was acting. He didn't seem the same. He became distant, quiet, and unhappy.

The boy soon realized it was wrong for him to have taken the wolf away from his environment. Because the wolf didn't know his *history,* his *role models,* and his *purpose for being,* he seemed to be wasting away. So the boy took him back to the woods. The boy tried to leave him, but the wolf wanted to follow. The wolf was domesticated and couldn't take care of himself. He couldn't hunt for food or protect himself. After days of the boy trying to teach him with no success, a pack of wolves came and tried to kill the gentle wolf. Why? Because the pack of wolves knew who they were. They knew their territorial and inherited rights through each generation teaching the next generation their character, their history, their traditions, and their purpose for existing.

But the wolf who had been raised among dogs did not know his creative ability through generational teachings. This was taken away from him by a boy who was only concerned about having his own household pet. As a result, the wolf lived in fear of the other wolves, but also lived in ignorance of his own creative ability.

One day, a female wolf came by and wanted to hunt with him. He wanted to impress her, so he did whatever she did — only better. After awhile, he started learning his creative ability and purpose, and soon became what God had called him to be.

The wolf was happy, and his purpose was fulfilled.

The Black Man is like that wolf who was taken out of his originally-intended environment. He was forced to live in an unnatural environment, and to become someone God didn't intend for him to be. *The Black Man must learn his biblical history and become that which God has intended for him to be, so that he is complete — so that the Body of Christ can be complete!*

Introduction —
The Lost Seed

What group of people currently composes 70 percent of the country's jail population? What group has been documented to show large numbers on drugs, men leaving their families, killing each other, stealing from one another, high unemployment rate, and having affairs outside of marriage? What group includes a large number of children never knowing their fathers? This group makes up six percent of the total population of America.

What group of people "for such a time as this" — a time when the return of Jesus is very near — is lost? The answer is the Black man. The world is predicting that, by the year 2000, 70 percent of the Black male seed will be dead, unemployed, or in prison.[1]

But this is not his true character, his purpose, his historical past — and it will not be his future.

> **For the Son of Man is come to seek and to save that which was lost.**
>
> **— Matthew 18:11**

For this present generation will make a difference in restoring back the Black male seed according to God's original purpose for his life.

It has been stated by Doctors William Berman and Dale Doty of the Christian Family Institute that this generation will use their families' pasts to strengthen their families' futures. The doctors agree that ancestry can play a role in how people live. They believe God intended us to use family

---

[1] *Tulsa World*, **Educator Fears for the Survival of the Black Male,** October 19, 1991.

history in genealogies described in both the Old and New Testaments, to shape our families' futures.[2]

Knowledge Is The Key

My people are destroyed for lack of knowledge.
— Hosea 4:6

Blacks are being destroyed for lack of knowledge — knowledge of the important part they played in history. Stripped of a heritage, without a culture, a biblical role model, or direction of purpose, as a *people* they misbehave like wayward children and are lost.

How think ye? If a man have an hundred sheep, and one of them be gone astray, doth he not leave the ninety and nine, and goeth into the mountains, and seeketh that which is gone astray?
— Matthew 18:12

Every race of people has a part to play in bringing Jesus back. For the Body of Christ has different parts — but all the parts are important in making the body complete.

If you have your doubts, consider what happens to the rest of your body when your heart stops beating. When your lungs collapse, consider what happens to your respiratory system.

We know the Father is the head of Jesus, and Jesus is the head of the Body of Christ. If Jesus leaves the Church, how long will the Body of Christ survive? (How long would you survive, apart from the Body of Christ?)

That there should be no schism in the body; but that the members should have the same care one for another. And whether one member suffer, all the members suffer with it; or one member be honoured, all the members rejoice with it.
— 1 Corinthians 12:25,26

---

[2]*Tulsa World*, **Authors Shake Your Family Tree**, November 24, 1991.

My purpose in writing this book is to give a race of people (Blacks) a knowledge and understanding of their culture and examples of Black biblical role models to follow, and to plant seeds of desire for Blacks to receive Jesus Christ into their hearts, so that they may seek God in prayer and in His Word. It is my desire that Blacks receive back their biblical heritage, so that they may no longer be tossed by every wind and doctrine. Instead, be changed into God's image — spirit, soul, and body — so that they would *know* their purpose and their place in the next move of God.

> **I alone know the plans that I have for you, plans to bring you prosperity and not disaster, plans to bring about a future you hope for. Then you will call to me, you will come and pray to me, and I will answer you. You will seek me and you will find me because you will seek me with all your heart.**
> **— Jeremiah 29:11-13 (GNB)**

1

Graven Images —
Man's or God's?

When you witness to the lost, do you take graven images of art and man's devices with you to bring others to salvation in Jesus Christ?

Are these graven images pictures of a blond-haired, blue-eyed, white-skinned Jesus? Take only the Word of God and His love — which is every skin color — and win the lost. Take Jesus and the Word of God so that they can see Jesus as they need Him to be — in their own image, in their own likeness, with their individual and physical characteristics — a Jesus Who can relate to every nation's heritage, culture, and unique personality.

Acts 17:29 says:

Forasmuch, then, as we are the offspring of God, we ought not to think that the God head is like unto gold, or silver, or stone *graven by art and man's device.*

Art work that has been painted or drawn by man's pencil or paintbrush to resemble Jesus is not of God but of man's imagination for his own form of worship.

Deuteronomy 4:12-16 says:

And the Lord spoke to you out of the midst of the fire: you heard the voice of the words, *but saw no form:* **there was only a voice.**

And He declared to you His covenant, which He commanded you to perform, the ten commandments; and He wrote them on two tables of stone.

And the Lord commanded me at that time to teach you statutes and precepts, that you might do them in the land which you are going over to possess.

> **Therefore take good heed to yourselves, since *you saw no form of Him* on the day the Lord spoke to you on Horeb out of the midst of the fire.**
> **Beware lest you become corrupt by making for yourself [to worship] a *graven image in the form* of any figure, the likeness of *male* or *female*.**

God does not want us corrupted by worshiping man's image of what God looks like: we are to live by the precepts He's given to each of us in the Word of God. True worshipers shall worship the Father in Spirit and in Truth.

Acts 17:30 says:

> **And the times of this ignorance *God* winked at: but now *commandeth all men everywhere to repent.***

Repent, and lay down graven artwork by man's devices so that you no longer worship an image of God, but worship Him in Spirit and in Truth, as God originally intended.

2

Who Are You?

Realize that [1]the American definition of a Black person is simple: any trace of Black characteristics in a person's body or lineage classifies that person as Black. Webster's Dictionary[2] defines a person of African descent as Negro, dark-skinned person of African origin; any person with Negro ancestors.

This study of the biblical heritage of the Black race will, therefore, use Webster's definition of who qualifies as Black.

Let me clearly state that this is not a racist book. The intent is to **seek and to save that which is lost** (Matthew 18:11). In this generation, the *lost* is the Black seed, the one who has no knowledge of his biblical history. Blacks must learn to see themselves as Christ sees them (complete and whole), knowing they are a valuable part of the Body of Christ — not more important than any other, but equally as important.

Blacks must not become racist, but complete in Jesus Christ. Whites must not become bitter, but complete their purpose in the Body of Christ.

There are those who believe that Ham was Black because he was cursed. The Bible states in Genesis 9:1 and 9:18 that *Ham was blessed*. What, then, is your reference point? Do not allow prejudice, racism, and the unfounded views and opinions of others to harden your heart. God's Word says that what God blesses, no man can curse.

---

[1]*The Black Presence in the Bible*, Rev. Walter Arthur McCray.
[2]*Webster's Dictionary*

Genesis 9:19 says:

> **These are the three sons of Noah and of them was the whole earth overspread. And God blessed Noah and his sons and said unto them, be fruitful and multiply and replenish the earth.**

Allow the Spirit of the Lord to discern biblical truths to you through prayer and reading God's Word; then let the Spirit of the Lord and common sense minister to you as you read this book, following along with your Bible.

3

Were You Represented In the Beginning?

In the beginning, God created the Garden of Eden which, in part, was in Africa. Genesis 2:10-14 says the river that went out of the Garden of Eden parted into four rivers.

The first was Pison, which surrounded Havilah, a country named and settled by Ham's grandson, Havilah (a Black man).

The second river is Gihon, which surrounded all of Ethiopia and is now known as the Nile River.[6d] In ancient times, "African" and "Ethiopian" meant the same thing — Black.[7b] In ancient Greek, Ethiopian meant *Black or sunburnt people.*[7b]

The third river was called Hiddekel, which "goeth toward the east of Assyria." The Assyrians were known to be dark people with a prominent nose whose hair, eyebrows and thick beard were bushy.[8] Assyria was originally settled, in part, by Blacks.[6d]

The fourth river is Euphrates, an area surrounded by land originally settled by Cushites (Blacks).

To geographically locate the ancient land of Cush, you must understand that the term "Cush" or "Ethiopia" meant where the Black descendants of Cush settled, which included parts of Africa and Asia.[7b] According to the 1884 edition of *The Family Bible* (pp. 1,3, by Beard and Dillon), Canaan was originally part of Africa (Ethiopia), all of which at a later period became independent.

Science and the Garden

A study by a University of California/Berkley molecular biologist, Dr. Allen Wilson, found conclusive genetic evidence that all people descended from a single African woman he named "Eve." Using DNA, the genetic blueprint of people, Dr. Wilson proved people descended from a woman who lived in Africa about 200,000 years ago.[1b,6d,6c] Other authors have stated that the history of Blacks began in Egypt (northern Ethiopia) and the Sudan (southern Ethiopia).[7b]

When God created the first man and the first woman in Africa, He named them Adam and Eve. One of their sons was Seth. Seth had a descendant named Noah. Noah had three sons. Ham was one of them (a Black man). The Bible calls Egypt "the land of Ham" (Psalm 78:51; Psalm 105:23-27; Psalm 106:21,22). Egypt and Ethiopia were historically called "the Land of the Blacks," or "Black Lands."[6d,6c,7b,8]

Some Bible dictionaries would try to interpret Egypt's meaning of "Black Land" as the color of the dirt. However, the Bible refers to Egypt as "the Land of Ham" — Ham meaning "a nation of Black people" (descendants of Ham) and not the color of the dirt.

Ham had four sons — Cush who settled Ethiopia, Mizraim, who settled Egypt; Phut, who settled Libya; and Canaan, who settled Canaan Land (the Promised Land, the "land of milk and honey"). The Bible states in Genesis 10:20, Ham's sons were the people who settled these lands by their families, by their languages, by their land, and by their nations.

The *New Unger's Bible Dictionary* states Cush, Mizraim and Phut set the pattern of the type of people, through direct ancestry, who settled Africa. *Unger's* also states that Canaan became the father of those that occupied Phoenicia and Palestine.

History Acknowledges Africans

Both Herodotus and Diodorus were great Greek historians. In Herodotus' writings, he wrote "the early Blacks were the most advanced of all the peoples" known to him. He did not hesitate to declare that their own European civilization has borrowed heavily from Africa, and that the Europeans had borrowed even more heavily in the field of religion.[7b]

The Bible is the written Word of God, inspired by the Holy Spirit and written by man. The Bible begins with, **In the beginning, God created the heavens and the earth** . . . (Genesis 1:1), and thus we have the beginning of the most historical book ever written. Notice the first two countries God mentions in the Bible are located in Genesis 2:11 and 13 Havilah, a country named after Ham's Black grandson (Genesis 10:7) and Ethiopia, a country settled by Ham's Black son, Cush.[7,8,8a,8b,6c,6d,8c,8d,8e] To go even further, Africa was among the first areas where Christianity spread. Religious concepts took place due to Jewish leaders in Africa. God told Abraham to separate himself from his country and his relatives unto a land He would show him. That land was a part of Africa — a land Abraham was to be a stranger in (Genesis 12:1,9,10; Genesis 17:8).

Joseph and his brothers journeyed to Egypt, a country in Africa (Genesis 37:28; Genesis 42:3; Genesis 45:17,18). Moses was not only born in Africa, but he was also married to the daughter of an African priest (Exodus 18:1). Mary and Joseph and baby Jesus fled to Africa, and remained there until the death of Herod, that it might be fulfilled which was spoken of the Lord by the prophet, saying, **Out of Egypt have I called my son** (Jesus) (Matthew 2:13-15).

The scientist, C. F. Volney, states in his book, *Voyage to Syria and Egypt.* (Paris: 1787) that the first Egyptians were "real Negroes of the same race as all the natives of Africa." It is generally noted because of mixing for many centuries among the Greeks and Romans that the Egyptians have lost much of their Black color; nevertheless, they still hold indesputable resemblance to their original ancestry.[6d]

The Greek, Herodotus, (484-425 B.C.) who is known as "the father of history," plainly described the Egyptians of his day as "burnt skinned, flat nosed, thick lipped, and wooly haired."[7b]

As you read this book, realize you were never an afterthought of God — but a part of God's original plan.

Chart 1

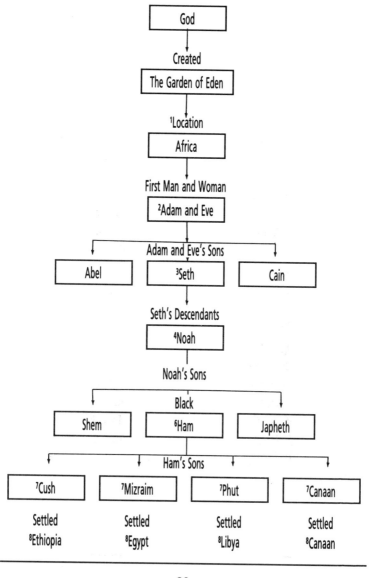

References

1 Genesis 2:9; Genesis 9:1-5,8,9,18-27
   a. Genesis 2:10-14
   b. "Adam and Eve Were Black." *Newsweek Magazine* (November, 1988)

2 Genesis 2:7,15; Genesis 1:26,27
   a. Genesis 1:28,31

3 Genesis 4:25, 5:3-29

4 Genesis 5:30

5 Genesis 8:4

6 Genesis 5:32; Genesis 7:13; Genesis 9:1
   a. *Harper's Bible Dictionary*, Madeleine S. Miller and J. Lane Miller
   b. Genesis 10:6-20; Genesis 10:21-31; Genesis 10:2-5
   c. *The Black Presence in the Bible*, Rev. Walter Arthur McCray
   d. *The Black Biblical Heritage*, John L. Johnson
   e. *W. Smith's Concise Dictionary of the Bible*

7 Genesis 10:6; 1 Chronicles 1:8
   a. "Was Cleopatra Black?" *Newsweek Magazine*. (September, 1991)
   b. *The Destruction of Black Civilization*, Chancellor Williams

8 *The New Unger's Bible Dictionary*
   a. *Harper's Bible Dictionary*
   b. "Ethiopian Kings," *National Geographic Magazine* (June, 1931)
   c. *The Black Jews of Harlem*, Howard Brotz
   d. *History of the Church in Africa*, Paul Marc Henry
   e. *Impact of the African Tradition on African Christianity*, Nya Kwiawon Taryor, Sr.

Chart 1a

Countries Settled By Noah's Sons

Synopsis

Noah's son, Ham, had sons, grandsons, and great-grandsons who originally settled the areas listed below.

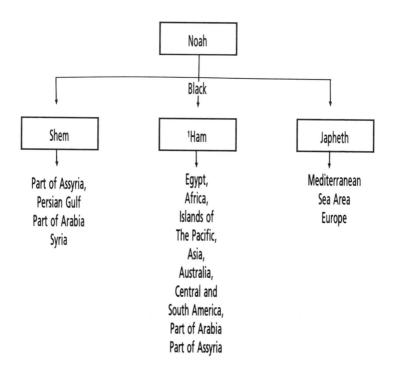

```
                    ┌──────────┐
                    │   Noah   │
                    └──────────┘
                       Black
   ┌──────────┬──────────────────┬──────────┐
┌──────────┐      ┌──────────┐      ┌──────────┐
│   Shem   │      │  ¹Ham    │      │ Japheth  │
└──────────┘      └──────────┘      └──────────┘
```

Shem	¹Ham	Japheth
Part of Assyria, Persian Gulf Part of Arabia Syria	Egypt, Africa, Islands of The Pacific, Asia, Australia, Central and South America, Part of Arabia Part of Assyria	Mediterranean Sea Area Europe

Reference
1 *The Black Biblical Heritage,* by John L. Johnson.

Chart 2

Synopsis

Ham had a son named Cush, who was the father of Ethiopia. The six men listed in Chart 2 were Ham's Black grandsons. Cush and his sons went on to settle China, India, and Afghanistan. Ethiopia is still predominantly Black.

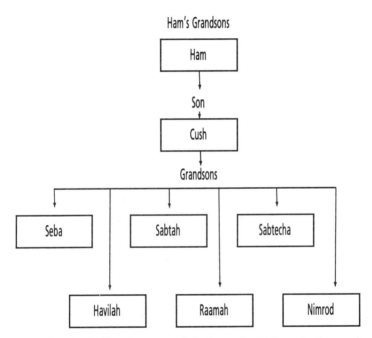

Ham's Grandsons

The Cush Empire extended through China, India, and Afghanistan. Cush means Cushite, Cushan, and Cushi.

References

The New Unger Bible Dictionary
Genesis 10:7; 1 Chronicles 1:19
Impact of the African Tradition on African Christianity, Nya Kwiawon Taryor, Sr.
The Black Biblical Heritage, by John L. Johnson

Chart 2a

Synopsis

Ham was the father of Cush and the grandfather of Seba. Seba's family was called "Sabean." It was the Sabeans who inhabited a kingdom in Western Arabia.

Seba – Ham's Grandson

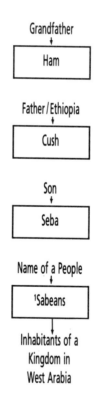

Grandfather

Ham

Father / Ethiopia

Cush

Son

Seba

Name of a People

[1]Sabeans

Inhabitants of a
Kingdom in
West Arabia

References
1 *The New Unger's Bible Dictionary*, Merrill F. Unger

Chart 2b

Synopsis

Ham's son, Cush, had a son named Havilah. He settled the Land of Havilah, which was inhabited by Ishmaelites and Amalekites.

Havilah — Grandson of Ham

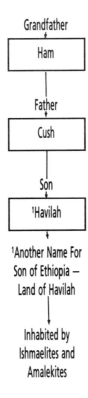

Grandfather

| Ham |

Father

| Cush |

Son

| ¹Havilah |

¹Another Name For
Son of Ethiopia —
Land of Havilah

Inhabited by
Ishmaelites and
Amalekites

References
1   Genesis 2:13; Genesis 10:7; Genesis 25:16-18
2   *The New Bible Dictionary*, J. D. Douglas

Chart 2c

Synopsis

Sabtah was the son of Cush and grandson of Ham, who is associated with Southern Arabia.

Sabtah / Cushites

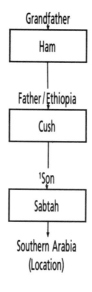

Grandfather

| Ham |

Father / Ethiopia

| Cush |

¹Son

| Sabtah |

Southern Arabia
(Location)

References

1 Genesis 10:7; 1 Chronicles 1:9
2 *The New Bible Dictionary*, J. D. Douglas

Chart 2d

Synopsis

Ham's son, Cush, had another son, Raamah. Ramaah had two sons, Sheba and Dedan. Sheba and Dedan settled Arabia. The Queen of Sheba came out of Sheba. She was a Cushite. Shem's grandson, Joktan, later came to Arabia and settled there after the Cushites originally settled the land.

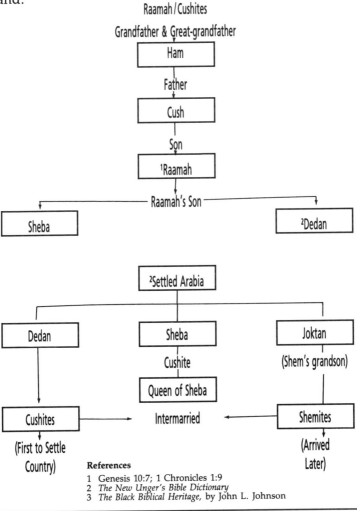

Raamah / Cushites

Grandfather & Great-grandfather

Ham

Father

Cush

Son

[1]Raamah

Raamah's Son

Sheba

[2]Dedan

[2]Settled Arabia

Dedan

Sheba
Cushite
Queen of Sheba

Joktan
(Shem's grandson)

Cushites
(First to Settle Country)

Intermarried

Shemites
(Arrived Later)

References
1 Genesis 10:7; 1 Chronicles 1:9
2 *The New Unger's Bible Dictionary*
3 *The Black Biblical Heritage*, by John L. Johnson

Chart 2e

Synopsis

Ham's son, Cush, had another son named Sabteca. Sabteca is associated with the tribes of Southern Arabia.

Sabteca / Cushites

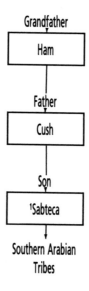

Grandfather

Ham

Father

Cush

Son

[1]Sabteca

Southern Arabian
Tribes

References

1 Genesis 10:7; 1 Chronicles 1:9
   The New Bible Dictionary, J. D. Douglas

Chart 2f

Synopsis

Ham had a grandson whose name was Nimrod. Nimrod means "mighty hunter before God." Nimrod settled a country called Shinar. The people of that country where called Sumerians. The chart below shows the Black kingdoms and Black cities Nimrod originally settled. Today, these geographic areas would be a part of Iraq.

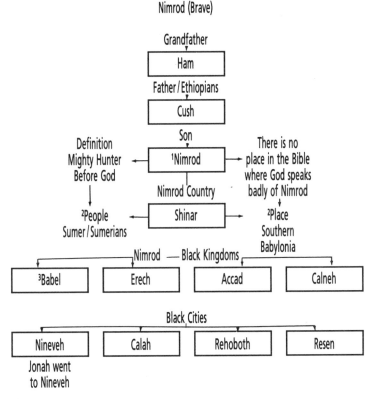

Nimrod (Brave)

Grandfather

Ham

Father / Ethiopians

Cush

Son

Definition
Mighty Hunter
Before God → [1]Nimrod → There is no place in the Bible where God speaks badly of Nimrod

Nimrod Country

[2]People
Sumer / Sumerians ← Shinar → [2]Place
Southern Babylonia

Nimrod — Black Kingdoms

| [3]Babel | Erech | Accad | Calneh |

Black Cities

| Nineveh | Calah | Rehoboth | Resen |

Jonah went
to Nineveh

References

1 *The Black Presence in the Bible,* Rev. Walter Arthur McCray
   Genesis 10:7-12
2 *The New Unger's Bible Dictionary.* Merrill F. Unger
3 Genesis 10:10-12
   The New Bible Dictionary, J. D. Douglas
   The Black Biblical Heritage, by John L. Johnson

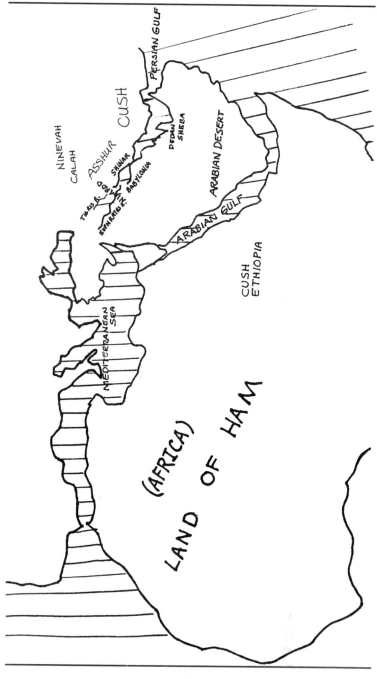

Chart 3

Synopsis

Ham had a Black son named Mizraim, who was the Father of Egypt (the Land of [2]Ham), a country he originally settled. And these seven Black men are Ham's grandsons.

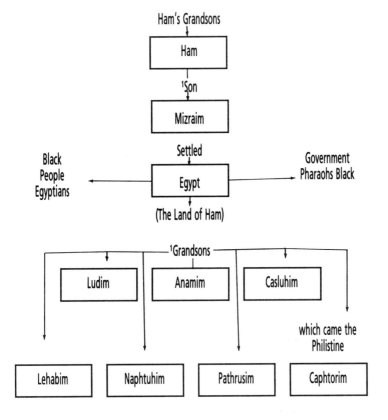

References

1 Genesis 10:13-14; Genesis 10:6
   History of the Church in Africa, Paul Marc Henry
   The Black Jews of Harlem, Howard Brotz
2 Psalm 78:51; Psalm 105:23,27; Psalm 106:21,22

Chart 3a

Synopsis

Ham's son, Mizraim, had a son named Ludim. The people were called Lydians who lived in Lydia, a country in Africa.

Ham's Grandson

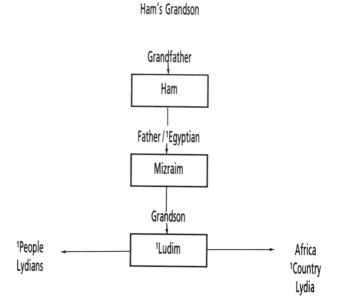

Grandfather

Ham

Father / [1]Egyptian

Mizraim

Grandson

[1]People
Lydians

[1]Ludim

Africa
[1]Country
Lydia

References

1 Genesis 10:13; 1 Chronicles 1:11
   The New Unger's Bible Dictionary, Merrill F. Unger.
   Impact of the Africa Tradition on African Christianity,
   Nya Kwiawon Taryor, Sr.

Chart 3b

Synopsis

Ham's son, Mizraim, had another son named Anamim. The people were called Anamites. They were an Egyptian tribe.

Ham's Grandson

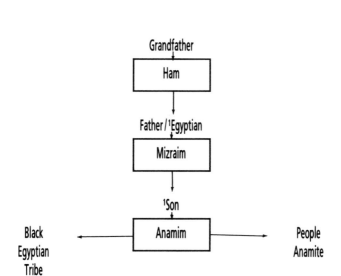

Grandfather

| Ham |

Father / ¹Egyptian

| Mizraim |

¹Son

Black Egyptian Tribe ← | Anamim | → People Anamite

References

1   Genesis 10:13; 1 Chronicles 1:11
    The New Unger's Bible Dictionary, Merrill F. Unger.

Chart 3c

Synopsis

Ham's son, Mizraim, had another son named Naphtuhim. The people were called Naphtuhites and were a Mizraite nation.

Ham's Grandson

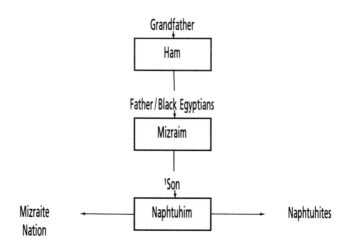

References
1 Genesis 10:13; 1 Chronicles 1:11

Chart 3d

Synopsis

Ham's son, Mizraim, had another son, Pathrusim. His people were called Pathrusites who settled Pathros.

Ham's Grandson

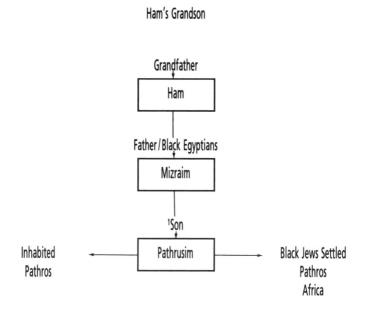

Grandfather

Ham

Father / Black Egyptians

Mizraim

¹Son

Inhabited Pathros ← Pathrusim → Black Jews Settled Pathros Africa

References

1 1 Chronicles 1:12
   The Black Jews of Harlem, Howard Brotz
   The New Unger's Bible Dictionary, Merrill F. Unger

Chart 3e

Synopsis

Ham's son, Mizraim, had another son named Casluhim. The people were called Casluhites.

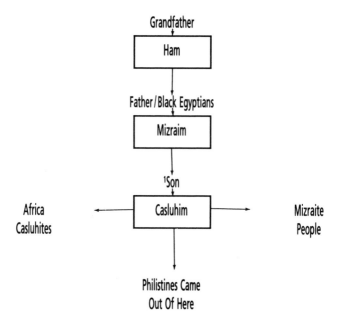

Ham's Grandson

Grandfather

Ham

Father / Black Egyptians

Mizraim

[1]Son

Africa
Casluhites

Casluhim

Mizraite
People

Philistines Came
Out Of Here

References

1   Genesis 10:14; 1 Chronicles 1:12
    The New Unger's Bible Dictionary, Merrill F. Unger

Chart 3f

Synopsis

Ham's son, Mizraim, had another son, Caphtorim. His people settled Caphtor or Crete in Egypt and were known as Sea People. They later migrated southwest of Canaan Land in the land of the Philistines. The cities listed below are the cities they originally settled.

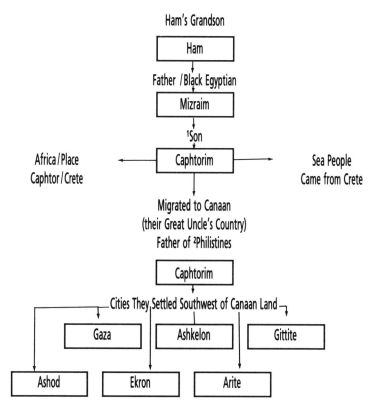

Ham's Grandson

| Ham |

Father / Black Egyptian

| Mizraim |

[1]Son

Africa / Place | Caphtorim | Sea People
Caphtor / Crete   Came from Crete

Migrated to Canaan
(their Great Uncle's Country)
Father of [2]Philistines

| Caphtorim |

Cities They Settled Southwest of Canaan Land

| Gaza | | Ashkelon | | Gittite |

| Ashod | | Ekron | | Arite |

References

1 1 Chronicles 1:12; Genesis 10:14
    The New Unger Bible Dictionary, Merrill F. Unger
*   *The most popular Black Philistines in the Bible are Delilah, and Goliath.*

Chart 4

Synopsis

Ham had another son named Phut. He settled the cities of Cyrene and Libya. Simon the Cyrenian played an important part in carrying Jesus' cross to Golgotha (see Mark 15:21,22).

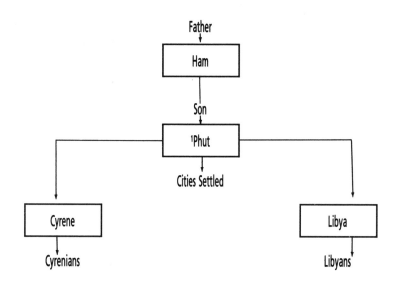

References

1 Genesis 10:6
   Harper's Bible Dictionary, s.v. "Cyrene."
   The New Unger's Bible Dictionary,
   The Black Biblical Heritage, by John L. Johnson

Chart 5

Synopsis

Ham had another Black son named Canaan. Canaan's sons, descendants and cities he settled are listed below. He also settled the cities listed below.

One of Jesus' disciples was Black — Simon, the Canaanite. He was a descendant of the Black man, Canaan.

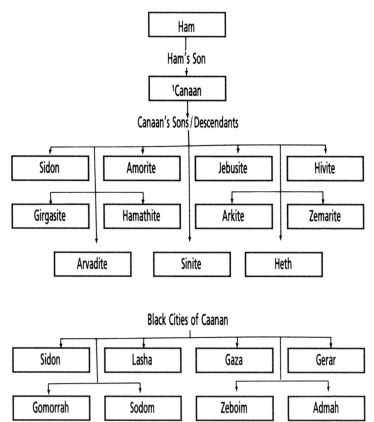

References

1 Genesis 10:15-19
    One of Jesus' Black disciples was Simon, the Canaanite.

Chart 5a

Synopsis

Ham's son, Canaan, had a son named Sidon. He settled the city of Sidon. His offspring were called Zidonians, or Phoenicians. They were peaceful craftsmen, merchants, and navigators. Some were hired by Solomon to help build the temple. The king of the Sidonians was Ethbaal, who worshiped Baal. His daughter, Jezebel, married Ahab. He was the seventh king of Israel. He was also in the lineage of Jesus.

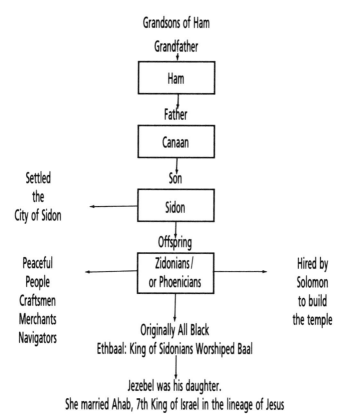

Grandsons of Ham

Grandfather

Ham

Father

Canaan

Son

Settled the City of Sidon ← Sidon

Offspring

Peaceful People Craftsmen Merchants Navigators ← Zidonians / or Phoenicians → Hired by Solomon to build the temple

Originally All Black
Ethbaal: King of Sidonians Worshiped Baal

Jezebel was his daughter.
She married Ahab, 7th King of Israel in the lineage of Jesus

References

1 Genesis 10:15; Genesis 10:19
   The New Unger's Bible Dictionary, Merrill F. Unger.

Chart 5b

Synopsis

Ham's son, Canaan, had a son named Heth. He was the forefather of the nation of Hittites. Esau and David married Hittites. The Hittites had huge armies who built high-walled cities to protect themselves.

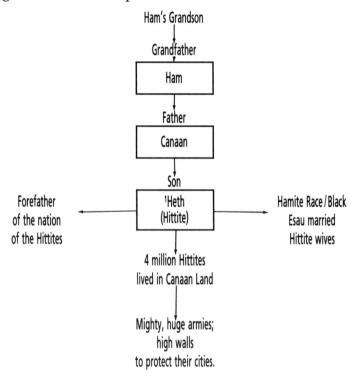

Ham's Grandson

Grandfather

Ham

Father

Canaan

Son

Forefather of the nation of the Hittites ← [1]**Heth (Hittite)** → Hamite Race / Black Esau married Hittite wives

4 million Hittites lived in Canaan Land

Mighty, huge armies; high walls to protect their cities.

References

1 Genesis 10:15; 1 Chronicles 1:13
  The New Unger's Bible Dictionary, Merrill F. Unger.
  The most popular Black Hittites in the Bible are Uriah and his wife, Bathsheba.
  David later married Bathsheba.

Chart 5c

Synopsis

Ham's son, Canaan, had another son named Jebus. His people were called Jebusites. They were used as bond-servants and keepers of the great temple in Zion. Jebus originally settled a city west of Jordan and named it Jerusalem.

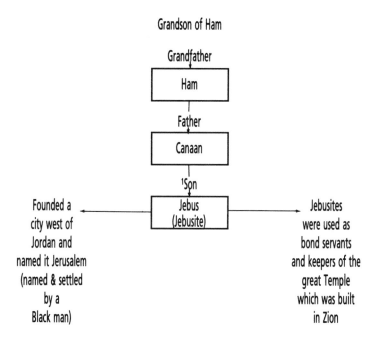

Grandson of Ham

Grandfather

| Ham |

Father

| Canaan |

¹Son

Founded a city west of Jordan and named it Jerusalem (named & settled by a Black man) ← | Jebus (Jebusite) | → Jebusites were used as bond servants and keepers of the great Temple which was built in Zion

References

1 1 Chronicles 1:14; Genesis 1:16
   The New Unger's Bible Dictionary, Merrill F. Unger
   The Black Biblical Heritage, by John L. Johnson

Chart 5d

Synopsis
Ham's son, Canaan, had a descendant named Amorite. They were called "Tall Ones." The first dynasty of Babylon was made up of Amorites.

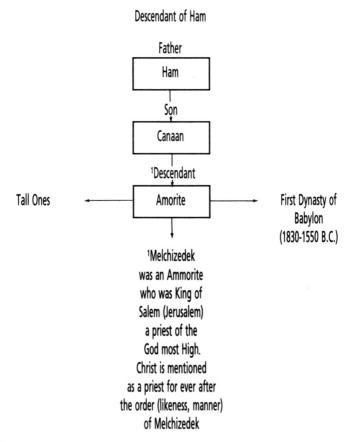

Descendant of Ham

Father

Ham

Son

Canaan

¹Descendant

Tall Ones ← Amorite → First Dynasty of Babylon (1830-1550 B.C.)

¹Melchizedek
was an Ammorite
who was King of
Salem (Jerusalem)
a priest of the
God most High.
Christ is mentioned
as a priest for ever after
the order (likeness, manner)
of Melchizedek

References

1 Genesis 10:16; Genesis 14:17-20; Hebrews 5:7
   The New Unger's Bible Dictionary, Merrill F. Unger
   Psalm 110:110:4
   C. W. Smith *Bible Dictionary*

Chart 5e

Synopsis
Ham's son, Canaan, had a descendant, Girgasite. They settled one of the nations of Canaan.

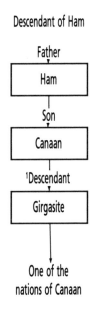

References
1 Genesis 10:16; 1 Chronicles 1:14

Chart 5f

Synopsis

Ham's son, Canaan, had a descendant named Hivite. The Hivites were warm-hearted. They were given to trade and to the multiplication of flocks and herds, rather than to war. They occupied the cities listed below.

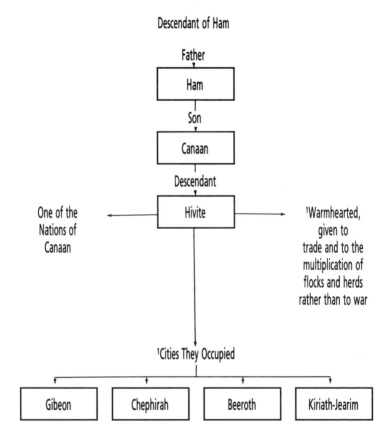

Descendant of Ham

Father

Ham

Son

Canaan

Descendant

One of the Nations of Canaan ← Hivite → [1]Warmhearted, given to trade and to the multiplication of flocks and herds rather than to war

[1]Cities They Occupied

| Gibeon | Chephirah | Beeroth | Kiriath-Jearim |

References

1 Genesis 10:17
   The New Unger's Bible Dictionary, Merrill F. Unger

Chart 5g

Synopsis

Ham's son, Canaan, had a descendant, Arkite. The Arkite people are the inhabitants of present-day Tel-Arka, which is 80 miles north of Sidon at the foot of Lebanon.

Descendant of Ham

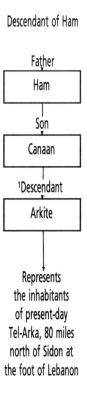

Father

Ham

Son

Canaan

¹Descendant

Arkite

Represents
the inhabitants
of present-day
Tel-Arka, 80 miles
north of Sidon at
the foot of Lebanon

References

1 Genesis 10:17; 1 Chronicles 1:15
   The New Unger's Bible Dictionary, Merrill F. Unger

Chart 5h

Synopsis

Ham's son, Canaan, had a descendant named Sinite. They settled the northern part of the Lebanon district. They are Sinites, or Sinim people. They may be associated with the tribe, Sina, in the Hindu-Cush (Lacouperie in Babylonian and Oriental records).

Descendant of Ham

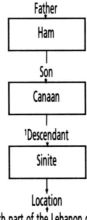

Father

Ham

Son

Canaan

[1]Descendant

Sinite

Location

North part of the Lebanon district

May be referred to as Sinim (remote people who would come to the light of Israel and of the Gentiles)

Referred to in Lacouperie, in Babylonian and Oriental records

References

1 Genesis 10:17; 1 Chronicles 1:15
   The New Unger's Bible Dictionary, Merrill F. Unger

Chart 5i

Synopsis

Ham's son, Canaan, had a descendant named Arvadite. They settled the island of Aradus, or Arnad, off the coast of Syria.

Descendant of Ham

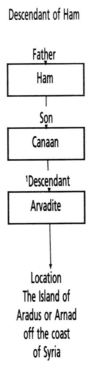

Father

Ham

Son

Canaan

[1]Descendant

Arvadite

Location
The Island of
Aradus or Arnad
off the coast
of Syria

References
1 Genesis 10:18; 1 Chronicles 1:16

Chart 5j

Synopsis

Ham's son, Canaan, had a descendant named Hamathite. They were the founder of Hamath.

Descendant of Ham

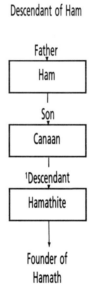

Father

Ham

Son

Canaan

¹Descendant

Hamathite

Founder of
Hamath

References

1   Genesis 10:18; 1 Chronicles 1:16
    The New Unger's Bible Dictionary, Merrill F. Unger

Chart 5k

Synopsis

Ham's son, Canaan, had a descendant named Zemarite. They settled the land between Arvad and Haneth.

Descendant of Ham

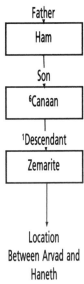

Father

Ham

Son

⁶Canaan

¹Descendant

Zemarite

Location
Between Arvad and
Haneth

References
1 Genesis 10:18; 1 Chronicles 1:16

Chart 51

Synopsis

The cities Canaan settled are listed below.

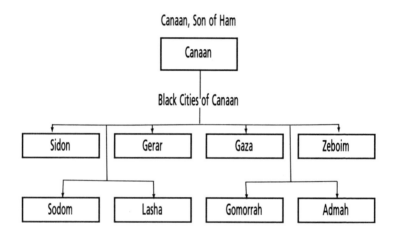

Reference
1   Genesis 10:15-19

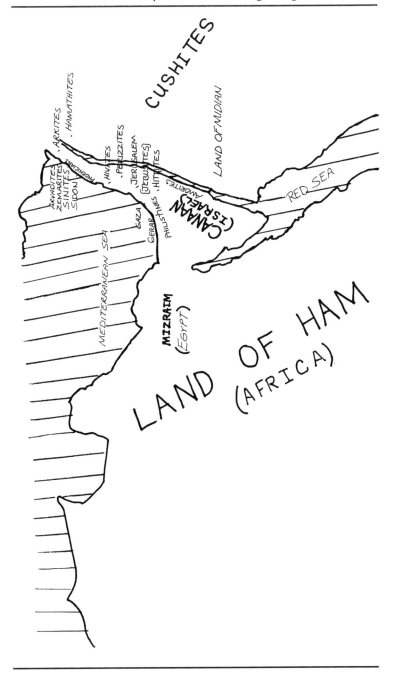

4
The Black Seeds of Abraham

Chart 1

Synopsis

Abraham married Sarah first — a woman of Shem's descent. After she died, Abraham married Keturah, of Hamitic descent (a Black Canaanite). Sarah had a handmaid named Hagar of Ham's descent (an Egyptian).

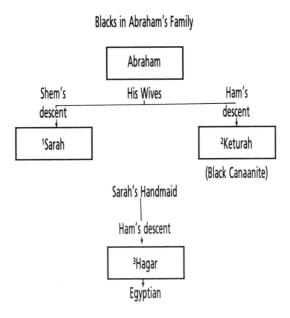

Blacks in Abraham's Family

References

1 Genesis 11:10,27
2 Genesis 25:1
3 Genesis 16:1-4

Chart 2

Synopsis

Abram's first son was conceived by Hagar (Ham's descent). The son was named Ishmael, and he was blessed. Afterwards, God changed Abram's name to ''Abraham'' (father of many nations). Ishmael later married a Black Egyptian woman.

After the birth of Ishmael,
God changed Abram's name
to Abraham —
Father of many nations.

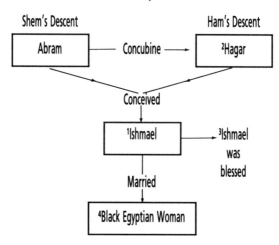

References

1 Genesis 16:15
2 Genesis 17:5
3 Genesis 17:20
4 Genesis 25:17,18

Chart 3a

Synopsis

Ishmael had a daughter, Mahaleth, and 12 Black sons. They were princes who ruled cities and nations.

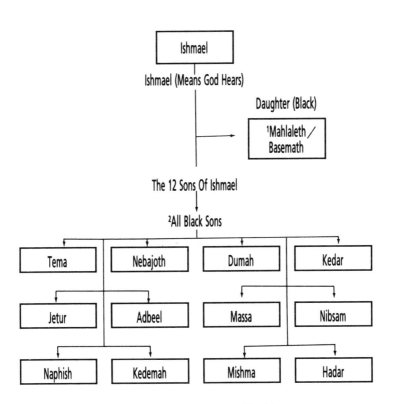

By their names, by their towns, and by their castles, they were 12 princes according to their nations.

References

1 Genesis 28:8,9
2 Genesis 25:12-16

Chart 3b

Synopsis

Ishmael's daughter, Mahaleth (Basemath), married Esau and they went to Edom and settled there. The people were called Edomites. Esau married three other women called Canaanites who were Black, and the sons Esau had by them were Black.

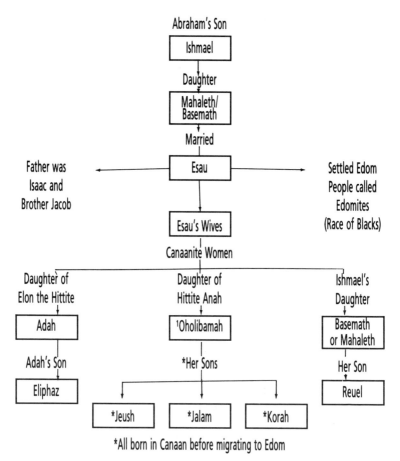

Ishmael's Daughter

Abraham's Son

Ishmael

Daughter

Mahaleth/Basemath

Married

Father was Isaac and Brother Jacob ← Esau → Settled Edom People called Edomites (Race of Blacks)

Esau's Wives

Canaanite Women

Daughter of Elon the Hittite	Daughter of Hittite Anah	Ishmael's Daughter
Adah	¹Oholibamah	Basemath or Mahaleth
Adah's Son	*Her Sons	Her Son
Eliphaz	*Jeush *Jalam *Korah	Reuel

*All born in Canaan before migrating to Edom

Reference
1 Genesis 36:1-19

Chart 3c

Synopsis

Esau's three wives had sons who later had grandsons who ruled the land of Edom.

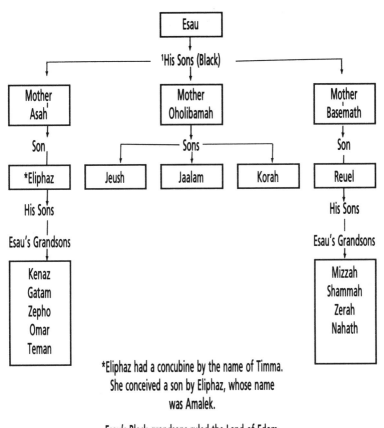

*Eliphaz had a concubine by the name of Timma. She conceived a son by Eliphaz, whose name was Amalek.

Esau's Black grandsons ruled the Land of Edom, divided by their Tribe names as Kings of Edom.

Reference
1 Genesis 36:10-19

Chart 4

Synopsis

Abraham married Keturah after Sarah's death. Keturah was Black, and had six sons by Abraham who were all Black. Abraham's Black sons had children, who made him a grandfather of Black children.

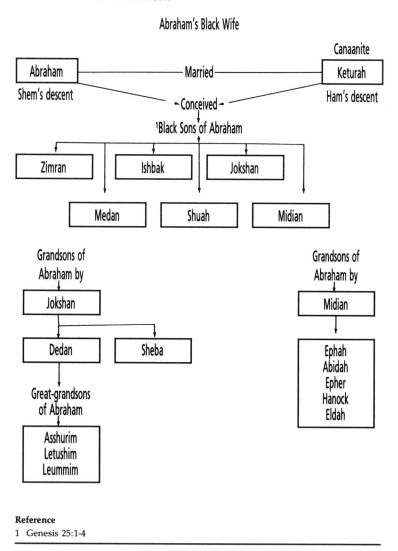

Abraham's Black Wife

Abraham — Married — Keturah (Canaanite)

Shem's descent — Conceived — Ham's descent

[1]Black Sons of Abraham

Zimran · Ishbak · Jokshan

Medan · Shuah · Midian

Grandsons of Abraham by Jokshan

Jokshan → Dedan · Sheba

Great-grandsons of Abraham → Asshurim, Letushim, Leummim

Grandsons of Abraham by Midian

Midian → Ephah, Abidah, Epher, Hanock, Eldah

Reference
1 Genesis 25:1-4

Chart 4b

Synopsis

Ham's son, Cush, had another son named Raamah. Raamah had two sons — Dedan and Sheba. Sheba settled the country of Sheba, where the Queen of Sheba reigned several generations later. She was a Black queen who came to visit Solomon at the temple in Zion.

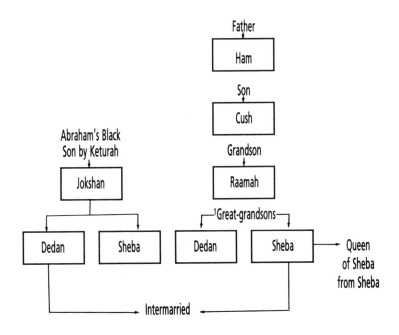

Both Settled Arabia
Produced a Race of Dark-Skinned People

References

1 *The New Unger's Bible Dictionary*, Merrill F. Unger
Genesis 10:6; Genesis 25:3

Chart 4c

Synopsis

One of Abraham's sons was Midian. Midian's mother was Keturah, of Ham's descent, which made Midian a Black man. Midian settled the country of Midian. The people were called Midianites. They were primarily merchants. When Moses killed the Egyptian, he fled to the land of Midian.

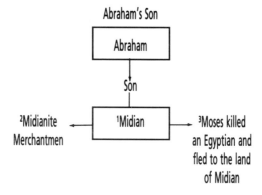

Abraham's Son

| Abraham |

Son

[2]Midianite Merchantmen ← [1]Midian → [3]Moses killed an Egyptian and fled to the land of Midian

References

1 Genesis 25:1,2
2 Genesis 37:25,27,28,36
3 Exodus 2:15

5
Moses' Black Family

Chart 1

Moses' Family

*[1]After Moses fled from Egypt,
he went to the Land of Midian*

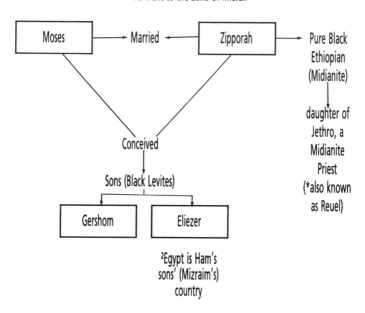

Moses → Married ← Zipporah → Pure Black Ethiopian (Midianite)

daughter of Jethro, a Midianite Priest (*also known as Reuel)

Conceived

Sons (Black Levites)

Gershom | Eliezer

[2]Egypt is Ham's sons' (Mizraim's) country

Moses delivered the Israelites out of a Black country (Egypt — Ham's descent) to a land of nothing but Blacks, the Land of Milk and Honey, where there were Canaanites, Amorites, Perizzites, Jebusites, Hittites, (Ham's sons and grandsons)

*Reuel means "Jethro"

References
1. Exodus 2:11-15; Exodus 2:15,16
2. Exodus 12:36-38

Chart 2

Synopsis

Joseph married a Black Egyptian named Asemath. They had two Black sons named Ephraim and Manasseh. Joseph's father, Jacob, adopted the grandsons as his own and blessed them.

Jacob's Son

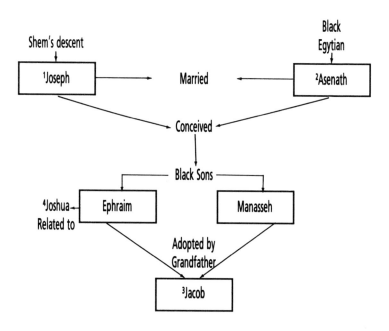

References

1 Genesis 41:45
2 Genesis 10:6
3 Genesis 48:1, 13-20
4 1 Chronicles 7:20-27

Chart 4b

Synopsis

Tamar, a Black Canaanite, and Judah conceived a son named Zara (Perez) in the lineage of Jesus. Rachab (or Rahab), a Canaanite harlot who assisted the Israelite spies when they came to spy out the Land of Milk and Honey. She received a blessing for this. She married Salmon and conceived a son named Boaz, who was in the lineage of Jesus. Bathsheba, a Black Hittite who married David, conceived a son name Solomon who is also in the lineage of Jesus.

Blacks in the Lineage of Jesus

```
            ┌─────────────────┐
            │      Adam       │
            └─────────────────┘
               Descendants
            ┌─────────────────┐
            │      Noah       │
            └─────────────────┘
           One of Noah's Sons
            ┌─────────────────┐
            │       Ham       │
            └─────────────────┘
            Noah's Grandson
            ┌─────────────────┐
            │     Canaan      │
            │  (Canaanites)   │
            └─────────────────┘
```

¹Tamar (or Thamar)		Judah
Black Canaanite	Conceived	

(Perez) ← Zara → (Black)

Salmon	Married ←	Rachab
	Conceived ←	(or Rahab) Black Canaanite harlot who helped the Israelite spies escape and was blessed

¹Boaz

(Black)

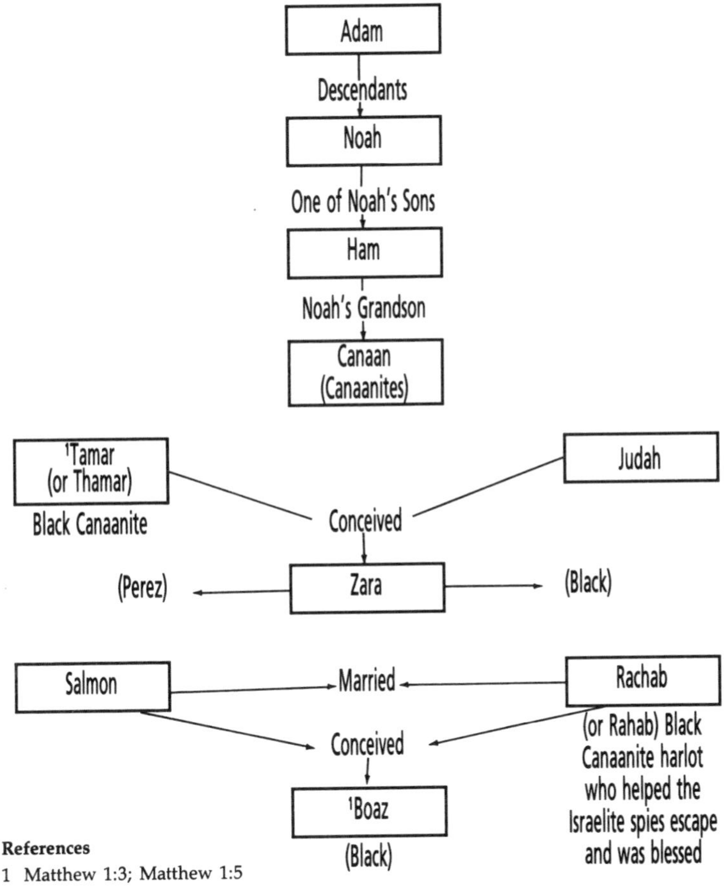

References
1 Matthew 1:3; Matthew 1:5

Chart 4c

Blacks in the Lineage of Jesus

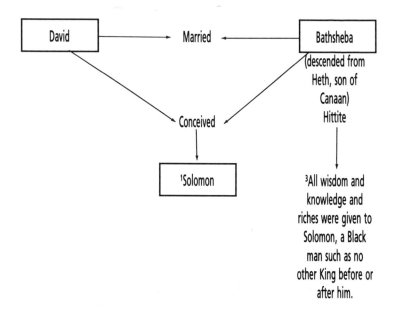

²Some of the generations' blood mixed with a race of Black people. The end result was Jesus — whose physical features are described only in the Books of Daniel and Revelations as "wooly haired, with arms and feet colored as brass, or feet colored as if burned from a furnace."

(Brass is yellowish, but when burned it is very dark — nearly Black.)

Genealogically speaking, Black ancestral blood ran in Jesus' human veins.

Romans 1:3 states . . . Concerning His son Jesus Christ, our Lord, which was made of the seed of David according to the flesh . . .

References

1 Matthew 1:6
2 Daniel 7:9; Daniel 10:6
3 1 Chronicles 1:7-12

A Summary of Some of the Decendants of Ham

1. Adam and Eve — Created by God in Africa. Anthropologists and scientists agree that human life began in Africa. They also agree that the first woman and man had Negroid characteristics.

2. Noah and His Wife — Born and raised in Africa. It is a scientific fact that they could not have had Ham, who was Black, without having some Black genes in either — or both — of their bloodstreams.

3. Ham — Means "Burnt" or "Black." Ham was not cursed; he was blessed by God.

4. Cush — Means Ethiopia; son of Ham.

5. Mizraim — Means Egypt; son of Ham.

6. Phut — Settled Libya; son of Ham.

7. Canaan — Canaanite; son of Ham.

8. Queen of Sheba — Cushite (Cush); from Ethiopia.

9. Nimrod — God did not record in the Bible that Nimrod was evil. God said Nimrod was a mighty hunter before the Lord, and Nimrod's people were in one accord. Therefore, nothing would be impossible for them (his people). Nimrod had a brilliant mind to organize, plan, and execute anything he set his hand to.

10. Uriah — Hittite soldier for David. He was a man of character, faithful to his people, and the ark of the covenant. He was faithful unto death.

11. Melchizedek — King of Salem (Canaanite); an Amorite of Ham descent: 1) high priest; 2) man of dignity; 3) man of peace; 4) a just man, full of righteousness.

12. Bathsheba — A beautiful Hittite woman whom David could not resist. Solomon's mother.

13. *Jebus* — son of Canaan; settled and named Jerusalem.

14. *Solomon* — Son of David and Bathsheba; man of wisdom, knowledge, and riches, in the lineage of Jesus.

15. *Keturah* — Canaanite (Abraham's wife).

16. *Hagar* — Abraham's concubine.

17. *Ishmael* — Abraham's first son.

18. *Mahaleth* — Ishmael's daughter who married Esau, Isaac's son.

19. *Zipporah* — Moses' wife, of the Midianites, a race of Blacks from Ethiopia.

20. *Asenath* — Joseph's wife, a Black Egyptian.

21. *Ephraim* — Mother was a Black Egyptian. His father was Joseph.

22. *Tamar* — Conceived a son by Judah; she was a Canaanite, and of the lineage of Jesus.

23. *Zara (Perez)* — Lineage of Jesus, mother was Tamar.

24. *Rachab (Rahab)* — Canaanite; married Salmon.

25. *Boaz* — Lineage of Jesus, mother was Rachab.

26. *Jesus* — Lord and Savior; a man of color with wooly hair. Jesus was not Hamitic, but Hamitic genes ran in His bloodline.

27. *Simon the Cyrene* — Helped Jesus to the cross; Cyrene was named and settled by Phut, Ham's son.

28. *Simon the Canaanite* — One of the 12 disciples.

29. *Simeon the Niger and Lucius of Cyrene* — They were teachers and prophets of the Antioch Church, established in Jerusalem; they ordained Barnabus and Saul by the Holy Ghost.

30. *The Eunuch* — A wealthy Black Ethiopian whom Phillip taught and baptized.

31. *Delilah* — Betrayed Samson. She was a Philistine from Crete (settled by Caphtorim, son of Mizraim).

32. *Goliath* — Was also a Black Philistine.

7

God's Black Forerunners

Melchizedek — The High Priest was the forerunner of God. Melchizedek gave Abraham bread and wine after Abraham's war victory. Abraham brought the tithe to Melchizedek, because he was likened unto Jesus — a type of Christ. Just as God offered up His son, Jesus, for a nation of people, Melchizedek prepared Abraham to offer up his son, Isaac, as a sacrifice for a nation of people. This was demonstrated in the communion of bread and wine.

Jethro (Black Midianite Priest) — Counseled Moses to teach representatives of each tribe. They counseled the people, so Moses would have the strength to go through the wilderness. Jethro was asked by Moses to help lead them out of the wilderness. For he was the eyes of God.

Nimrod (Mighty Hunter Before God) — The Ethiopian was used of God to teach his people how to build a civilization (Babal) and live as a civilized nation. He taught people what they could do if they were in one accord. Although God divided their language because they did not serve God, other civilizations were begun.

Rachab (Rahab) — Canaanite harlot; helped the two spies escape, who were a part of the next move of God when the walls of Jericho came down.

Simeon the Niger — Teachers and prophets of the Antioch Church who prayed and laid hands on Barnabus and Saul and launched them out on their ministry.

Ananais — Who prayed and laid hands on Saul of Tarsus so he could see again. And this was the beginning of Saul's ministry as Paul, the Apostle.

Simon the Canaanite — One of Jesus' 12 disciples, who Jesus launched out to minister to the world.

The Eunuch — The Ethiopian who, after being baptized by Phillip, evangelized a whole nation of Ethiopians.

Simon of Cyrene — Jews (Shemites) accused Jesus. Romans (Japhethites) sentenced Jesus to death; and Hamites (Black) helped Jesus carry His cross to Calvary. An angel appeared to the people who saw Jesus ascend to heaven. The angel asked why the people were looking up — *"For He shall return in the same manner that He left."* Shemites, Japhethites and Hamites sent Jesus to the cross, and it is going to take Shemites, Japhethites, and Hamites (Black) to bring Him back for a complete church.

William J. Seymour — (1900) — The Pentecostal Movement has emerged as one of the most important movements in the 20th century, due to a Black man who was used by God powerfully at 321 Azusa Street. The revival, which lasted several years — day in, day out — is credited for reintroducing the Holy Spirit to the Church.

Martin Luther King, Jr. — He had been to the mountain top; he had seen the coming of the glory of the Lord. He was a prophet of God who preached to all nations peace, love, and non-violence. He was used of God, called of God, and anointed of God to preach peace.

Who will be ready for the next move of God?

Why It Is Important For the Black Man To Receive Back His Identity and His Heritage

Verily, verily, I say unto you. He that believeth on me, the works that I do shall he do also; and greater works than these shall he do; because I go unto my Father.

— John 14:12

Since we believe that in order to do the works that Jesus did, we must first know what those works were, how do we learn? By studying the history of Jesus, learning about His character, His purpose and His ministry on the earth. The greater works will come when we recieve the Holy Spirit, and the power through Jesus Christ.

God is not color-blind. He looked down at His creation on the earth and saw the white clouds, the blue sky, the different colors of all the other animals, and the beautiful shades of all flowers. And He said, *"It is good!"* The trees that turn from brown to green to orange to yellow and then brown again are all His creation.

He created the whole world, and its many colors, for a purpose. God has never, nor will He ever, do anything without having a purpose for doing it. When He created trees, He did not create them to all look alike. Different trees have different appearances, colors, shapes, and purposes. An apple tree bears apples. A palm tree bears coconuts. The redwood tree provides shade and industrial uses. An apple tree cannot produce figs. A black grizzly bear cannot decide to act like a Koala. Think of the branches he would break if he tried to climb as the Koala does!

God created each of them — with different colors, different attributes, and different purposes.

When He created man, God did not become color-blind. He did not say, "I know no color in people!" What He said was, **"I am no respector of persons."** Being no respector of persons does not mean that God does not see race or color. It means that even though people are of different races and colors, they are *all equal* in God's eyes, with different purposes for existence.

Just as the Body of Christ has different members, they are all equally important with different purposes. One member, one part, one color is not more important than another but exists for a different purpose to complete the whole. All are necessary.

People of color — do not let people tell you that your color is not important. God does not do anything without having a purpose for it. God is an unchanging God. The same purpose He had for you in the Bible (in His unchanging nature) is the same purpose He has for you now.

You Are Descendants of Ham

You are descendants of Ham. Your forefathers were the eyes of God and forerunners of God in the Bible. And so are you this day — the next move of God!

To know the history of Jesus is important for you to become spiritually. To know your history biblically is important for you to become naturally.

God works with the spiritual and the natural together. So shall it be for you to be complete.

God needed a natural body to breathe life (spiritually) into Adam. God spoke to the dry bones and added muscles, nerves and skin first — then added the breath of life (spiritually). Jesus could not come to the earth without a natural body first. At the age of 30, the Holy Spirit descended upon Him, and He began his three-year ministry.

Your natural body is here for a purpose. The Holy Spirit will enable you to do what God has called you to do.

So, Black man — God has not called you to kill each other, shoot up drugs, leave your wives and children, and depend on the government for handouts. He has called you to be the eyes of God, and the forerunners of the next move of God.

How do you do that? You learn who your biblical ancestors are. Learn their contributions and their character. Accept who they are and what they did in history, knowing that God is an unchanging God. Their purpose is your purpose if you are to become what God has called you to be!

Follow These Examples

Melchizedek was King of Salem. Even though it is not recorded who his mother and father were, Melchizedek could look down at his skin and see that it was Black — a descendant of Ham. It is the same with adopted children who don't know who their parents are: they can look at their skin and tell what color they are, so that much of their heritage is established.

Melchizedek was a high priest.

Black man — become a man of respect, as was *Melchizedek*. He was a man of dignity, peace, and righteousness. Become that man of dignity, peace, and righteousness. Don't be a man who starts wars, fights, killings, hatred, and bitterness: be a man who brings peace to all nations.

Jethro was a Black Midianite priest. He was Moses' father-in-law, and Moses looked to him as a counselor. He guided Moses and the Israelites out of the wilderness.

Black man — be a counselor to your children. Become someone they can come to for help. Counsel your brothers and sisters of all nations so that they can complete the plan of God. Guide your family out of poverty, lack, low self-esteem, and failure. Guide them into God's purposes for their lives.

Solomon was the son of King David and Bathsheba, the Black Hittite. God gave him all wisdom to rule his people. God told Solomon that there was never a man richer, nor would there ever be any man richer than he was.

Solomon was a Black man, and God gave him all wisdom and wealth. God put most of the wealth of the world in Africa. He told Abraham to give his tithes to Melchizedek, a Black man. The best place to live in the days of the Bible was a Black country named Canaan.

Isn't it time, Black man, for you to walk in that wisdom and possess the wealth and riches that God originally put into your land to inherit?

Uriah the Hittite was a descendant of Ham and King David's best soldier. He was loyal to his king, faithful, and protective of the ark of the covenant. Always concerned for his men on the battlefield, he was a man of strength and character.

Black man — be the best at whatever you do that is of God. Be loyal to your employer. Keep God first at all times in everything you do. Help your fellow Black brothers and sisters become what God has called them to be. Help your family, your neighbor, your race: then you can make a difference.

Be a man of character, a family man, a man who is faithful to his wife and who provides for his family.

Nimrod was a mighty man before God and a descendant of Ham. Nimrod had a brilliant mind. He planned and organized his people to build a tower in Babel to reach heaven. God was impressed at how all his people worked together in one accord, and because of this, nothing would be impossible to them.

Black man — God has given you the ability to plan, organize, and execute anything you put your hands to do through Jesus Christ. Your people can be in one accord and work together. But you must teach them what you know. And through Jesus Christ, it will happen.

You Are Black
For God's Own Purposes

Your color denotes your purpose. But God does not favor you over any other race of people. He sees you in your color, along with other races of people in their colors. All are fulfilling God's purpose with equal importance.

Each race of people must do their part in the Body of Christ in order for it to work as One, and to usher in the return of Jesus Christ.

So, Black man — know who you are, become who you are. *You are part of the next move of God!*

8

Are You Part of
God's Plan?

This book introduces you to a very few of the Hamite descendants in the Bible. I encourage you to study and seek out Blacks in the Bible and discover the roles they played in each move of God.

You must also become the person God has called you to be (the eyes of God) (Numbers 10:31).

God wants you to be whole in Him — spiritually, physically, mentally, socially, and financially.

But the only way to know the Father is through Jesus Christ, His Son. You must believe that Jesus is the Son of God. You must believe that He died for your sins and was raised from the dead on the third day. He is seated at the right hand of the Father in heaven. If you believe this and if you want to be changed into the man or woman God has always intended you to be, pray this prayer with me out loud:

Father, I believe that Jesus died for my sins and was raised from the dead so that I might have life and have it more abundantly. Forgive me of my sins and I believe, by faith, that You do forgive me.

Come into my heart and be Lord over my life — spiritually, physically, socially, and financially. I thank You for Your purpose in my life and I determine in my heart to become that which You created me to be — a person of dignity, righteous like Melchizedek, with the character and honor of Uriah the Hittite, and the wisdom, knowledge and wealth like Solomon. In Jesus' mighty name, AMEN.

To Order

My People

or for more information about the author,

write

Fowler Enterprises

P. O. Box 1327

Tulsa, OK 74101

Price: $7.95 per copy plus 7½% tax
and $2.50 shipping and handling
(Add 50 cents shipping for each additional copy.)

Please include:

Name _____

Address _____

_____ Zip_____

Telephone _____

Please enclose your check or money order as payment.